IDENTITY DILEMMAS: THE CONSEQUENCE OF IDENTITY IN PROTRACTED CONFLICT

The nature of the case first compelled us to advance our empire to its present height; fear (*deos*) being our principal motive, though honor (*timê*) and interest (*ôphelia*) afterwards came.

Athenian Envoy Speech to the Spartan Assembly
—Thucydides

Introduction

Conflict is endemic to humanity. The principal motives for conflict remain, as Thucydides observed during the Peloponnesian War over two thousand years ago, fear, interest, and honor.[1] It can be argued that this triad of core motives captures the underlying causal factors present in most belligerent contests. While more than one of these motives may be at work in any given conflict, a single motive can and often does outweigh the others. This primary motive must be identified and addressed to truly resolve the conflict in question. Culture influences the magnitude of the motives and thus provides a lens through which to discern the motives at work. A potential solution emerges once it is known whether the positions in conflict are taken predominantly out of fear, interest, or honor. If interests can be identified, then they can be appeased. Fears, once recognized, can be eased. However, honor, once besmirched, is not easily assuaged.

This examination contends that honor, the most difficult of the three motives to accurately assess and adequately address, frequently outweighs fear and interest in the prolongation of human conflict. As Richard Lebow, drawing from ancient and modern philosophy, concludes in his ambitious theoretical departure entitled *A Cultural Theory for International Relations*:

The active pursuit of honor and standing by individuals and states is often costly... Foolhardy feats in battle, accepting war under unfavorable circumstances or building battle fleets that needlessly provoke a conflict with another major power indicate that honor and standing are not infrequently pursued at significant cost to security.[2]

Honor, a primal code of human behavior, plays a powerful role in war and, therefore, has a pivotal role to play in peace.

With the three paradigms of international relations theory as foundation and Lebow"s underappreciated departure as inspiration, this study seeks to advance the Thucydidean triad as a basis for analyzing conflict. It begins with the realist view and the role of fear in violent clashes. Next, it adds the liberalist view and interest as a core motive underlying conflict and cooperation. It then overlays the constructivist view of the world, highlighting the significance of culture and the centrality of honor in the continuation of conflict. Having described the motives, the study distills the fear-interest-honor triad into a security-prosperity-identity framework for analyzing conflict. It then applies this analytic framework to three of the world"s most intractable conflicts—Israel-Palestine, India-Pakistan, and China-Taiwan—to discover the weight of the motives presently at work. Drawing conclusions from the findings, the study offers recommendations for analyzing and resolving such conflicts.

Fear, Interest, and Honor

Though character and conduct vary, there are discernable constants in war. Beginning with the ancient Greeks, historians and philosophers uncovered these constants for posterity. Whether to preserve experience, prescribe method, or promote thought, the contributions of Thucydides, Plato, Aristotle, Hobbes, Locke, Kant and others offer penetrating insight into the saga of human conflict and cooperation. Such works stand the test of time and inform modern international relations theory chiefly

2

because the underlying motives of individual human behavior, as originally described by the Greeks and amplified by others, are the underlying motives of collective human or state behavior. In other words, the behavior of states, as human constructs, reflects the behavior of humans.

While Thucydides is considered the father of realism, all three prominent theories of international relations—realism, liberalism, and constructivism—are eloquently reflected in his above-stated triad of Athenian motives. In the anarchical system of realism, security (fear) is a primary motive for competition between state actors. In the interdependent system of liberalism, prosperity (interest) is a primary motive for cooperation between state and supra-state actors. In the ideational system of constructivism, identity (honor) is a primary motive for competition and cooperation between both state and non-state actors. All three schools of thought have merit. Moreover, all three are consistent with the introductory epigram and the analytical framework advanced by this study. This section of the study examines and applies realism, liberalism, and constructivism in successive layers to highlight the salience and significance of security, prosperity, and identity as underlying motives in the behavior of states in conflict. These motives, it may be surmised, are derived from the physical, material, and social needs that shape the behavior of actors at all levels.

Realism and Fear. In the profoundly influential book on political thought, *Leviathan*, Thomas Hobbes asserts, "Out of civil states, there is always war of every one against every one."[3] According to Hobbes, the competitive nature of man predisposes him to war.[4] Focusing on man"s immutable nature, the realists, led by Morgenthau, view states as unitary actors aggressively competing against one another

3

for power in an anarchical environment.[5] Neorealists redefined this competition as one for security. According to neorealist theory, the ultimate concern of states is not power but security.[6] Kenneth Waltz contends, "In an anarchic domain, a state of war exists if all parties lust for power. But so too will a state of war exist if all states seek only to ensure their own safety."[7]

In this arena, physical survival is the overriding imperative, and psychological fear is the underlying motive. An action by one state to make itself more secure makes others less secure. Fearing the one, the others then take steps to make themselves more secure. In this security dilemma, the actions taken to increase security may make all parties less secure.[8] In such an environment, fear or apprehension (*deos*) abounds.[9] According to Waltz, "Preoccupation with identifying dangers and counteracting them become a way of life. Relations are tense; the actors are usually suspicious and often hostile even though by nature they may not be given to suspicion and hostility."[10]

In the case of the Peloponnesian War, the growth of Athens" power caused fear in the Sparta-led Peloponnesian League. According to Thucydides, "The growth of Athens, and the alarm which this inspired in Sparta, made war inevitable."[11] The two powers were caught in a security dilemma. Many states since have been caught in such a dilemma. Yet, as Joseph Nye and David Welch note, war, while probable in this environment, is not inevitable.[12] Cooperation between the two was possible and, as Robert Axelrod, applying game theory, demonstrates in *The Evolution of Cooperation*, was arguably preferable to the devastation caused by decades of war.[13]

Liberalism and Interest. In *The Second Treatise of Government*, the father of liberalism, John Locke, writes:

> To avoid this state of war is one great reason of men's putting themselves into society, and quitting the state of nature: for where there is an authority, a power on earth, from which relief can be had by appeal, there the continuance of the state of war is excluded, and the controversy is decided by that power.[14]

The anarchic environment and the constant threat of war necessitate cooperation. The philosophical precursors for liberalism may be found in Locke"s *Two Treatise of Government* (quoted above) and Immanuel Kant"s "Perpetual Peace." In the latter, Kant argues that, "A state of peace... must be *established* [emphasis in original]... in order to be secured against hostility."[15] In essence, anarchy necessitates society. States place themselves into society, submitting to international norms and institutions out of mutual fear and mutual interest.

Absolute gain can be achieved through international cooperation. According to liberalists, material gain or profit (*ôphelia*), the same material interests that motivated Athens to eventually conflict with Sparta, motivate states to cooperate with each other. The premise, advanced by Adam Smith in *The Wealth of Nations,* that free trade benefits all parties is a fundamental tenet of liberalist thought. Trade agreements and supra-state organizations, such as the General Agreement on Tariffs and Trade and the 153-member World Trade Organization, exist today to liberalize international commerce and thereby improve the prosperity of all signatory and member states. Through such arrangements, absolute gain is supposed to trump relative gain.

Athens was motivated by absolute gain in cooperating with the city-states of the Delian League. A mutual threat—Persia—and a mutual interest—commerce—bound the members of the league together. In return for protection from Persia, Athens, the strongest city-state, sought relative gain in the form of tribute from less powerful members of the alliance. In this case, what began as cooperation became competition as Athens, forcefully imposing its will to satisfy its interests, grew heavy-handed in the administration of the league, subjugating and extorting other members. Prior to the start of the Peloponnesian War, Athens, warring with Persia, conquered much of Greece, and the Delian League became the Athenian Empire. In time, Athens" predatory pursuit of tribute posed a threat to the Peloponnesian League.

As James Nathan asserts in *Soldiers, Statecraft, and History: Coercive Diplomacy and International Order*, the forceful imposition of will threatens the autonomy of states and the regional balance of power.[16] The use of coercive force provokes a vigorous and often violent backlash from those being threatened. Athens was no exception. Its hegemonic behavior, motivated in large part by material interests, posed a threat to other city-states; insurrections broke out and war ensued. However, as Thucydides succinctly observes and Lebow vigorously upholds, the ancient Greeks" conduct was also motivated by honor. Honor, perhaps more than any other core motive, prolonged the clash between the Greek city-states. At the risk of being labeled reductionistic, this examination boldly contends that honor remains a primary cause of and offers a potential solution to protracted human conflict.

Constructivism and Honor. Constructivists challenge realism"s convictions regarding fear as well as liberalism"s conclusions regarding interest and contend that the behavior of states as social constructs is also governed by culture. Culture may be described as a range of learned behavior patterns. The cultural values that govern interaction and shape identity at the individual level also govern interaction and shape identity at the collective level. In the constructivist view, nurture outweighs nature at the individual and the collective level of behavioral analysis. As Jeffrey Lantis notes in his examination, "Broadly speaking, scholars contend that political culture has both anthropological origins—in language, religion, customs, and socialization—and historical origins in shared experiences (and the interpretation of common memories)."[17]

According to the prominent constructivist scholar Alexander Wendt, behavior at the international level, like behavior at the individual level, is influenced by interaction with others. Wendt contends that "To analyze the social construction of international politics is to analyze how processes of interaction produce and reproduce the social structures—cooperative or conflictual—that shape actors" identities and interests and the significance of their material contexts."[18] Behavior, according to Wendt, is not static; it changes, through a process of social interaction, over time. Culture can thus be defined as a dynamic set of behavioral norms and values derived from shared anthropological, historical, and social experiences.

In *A Cultural Theory for International Relations*, Lebow presents a penetrating, though occasionally pedantic, theory on the human logics that govern conflict and cooperation. He posits three fundamental motives—reason, appetite, and spirit—that influence behavior at individual and collective levels. Simply stated, when there is an imbalance among the motives and reason fails to constrain either appetite (interest) or spirit (honor), actors behave in ways that threaten others. Tensions escalate and fear, a fourth motive, begins to govern behavior.[19] While Lebow"s painstaking work informs this examination, the focus of this study is on conflict rather than cooperation. Fear, interest, and honor, rather than reason, dictate the behavior of actors in conflict.

Lebow gives special emphasis to the impact of honor on individual and state behavior because, as he attests, "the motive is more or less ignored by political science."[20] In addition to being ignored, special emphasis is placed on it here because honor often outweighs the other motives in the instigation, prolongation, and, moreover, the termination of conflict. Drawing on the writings of Homer and Thucydides, Lebow develops an ideal-type honor-based society.[21] Homer"s *Iliad* played a central role in ancient Greek education and the development of Greek values.[22] Lebow characterizes the ancient Greeks as a society based largely on honor.

Lebow writes, "The Greeks were fed Homer with their mother"s milk, and nowhere was the diet so rich as in Sparta, where respect for the past and its values was actively fostered by the state."[23] Given the premise of the present study, his description of such societies is instructive and warrants restating in full:

> In honor-based societies, honor cannot be attained without risk, so leaders and followers alike welcome the opportunity to risk limbs and lives to gain or defend it. Risk-taking will be extended to the defense of material possessions. Risk-taking actors will also defend their autonomy at almost any cost because it is so closely linked to honor, unless they can find some justification for disaggregating it from honor that is convincing to themselves and their peers.[24]

Honor (*timê*) was one of the most important values in ancient Greek society and an integral part of the Spartan identity. No value carried more weight.

Honor appears to have outweighed fear and interest in Sparta"s decision to declare war on Athens. Athens and Corinth, an ally of Sparta, were engaged in a conflict over Corinth"s colony at Potidaea. The Corinthians blamed Athens" aggressive actions on Sparta"s passive inaction.[25] The Corinthians charged their allies, the Spartans, with failing to stand with them against the escalating Athenian hostility.[26] Corinth questioned Sparta"s commitment to the alliance and by doing so questioned Sparta"s honor. In light of these accusations, failing to come to the aid of its ally would have been highly dishonorable.[27] Athens" belligerent behavior was perceived as an affront to Sparta"s dignity. Lebow concludes that "The Spartan decision for war was not motivated by concern for physical security but by ontological security: the need to defend Spartan values and identity.[28] This motive is not unique to the Spartans. As others note, honor and its opposite, shame, are inseparable from the human condition.[29] These opposing poles exert a powerful force on human behavior yet are largely undervalued in examining the behavior of states.

Honor, which Lebow equates with the spirit, "is the universal human need for self-esteem."[30] Self-esteem is closely related to identity. Identity, a social psychology term, refers to the distinctive image of self held and projected by an actor.[31] It is formed over time through interactions with others and reflects the culture of the actor"s environment.[32] Identity, although gaining credibility, is perhaps the least understood and most underrated stimulus considered by contemporary international relations theorists.

Three principal catalysts may be deduced from the major paradigms of international relations theory: security, prosperity, and identity. These three catalysts correspond to the constants—fear, interest, and honor—originally articulated by Thucydides. In employing Thucydides" elegant triad and endorsing Lebow"s exceptional theory, this essay seeks to underscore the importance of fear, interest, and, above all, honor as motives for conflict. The following section converts the fear-interest-honor triad into a security-prosperity-identity framework for assessing the behavior of states in conflict.

The Triad as a Framework

Concise definitions are useful for constructing a practical framework. In the framework put forth here, the triad of motives described above forms the basis of a state"s actions. To sum, three types of innate human needs—physical, material, and

9

social—drive individual and collective behavior. The state, as a collective human construct, is driven largely by its security, prosperity, and identity needs. Consequently, the behavior of the state, can be characterized as fear-, interest-, or honor-based. Actions taken to maintain or enhance security are fear-based actions; actions intended to maintain or enhance prosperity are interest-based actions; actions taken to maintain or enhance identity are honor-based actions.[33] A single action may, however, serve more than one motive and satisfy more than one goal. Nevertheless, a single motive can and often does outweigh the others.

Accurately identifying this motive, while key to understanding the conflict in question, can be difficult to do. Most scholars, including Thucydides, believe Sparta"s decision to declare war on Athens was motivated by fear.[34] Yet, as Lebow deftly demonstrates, the proximate cause of Sparta"s decision to attack Athens was Corinth"s scathing rebuke.[35] Sparta, as leader of the Peloponnesian League, was compelled less by fear than by honor. Sparta, with its renowned military prowess, was expected to defend the league. As previously established, Sparta"s identity was threatened.[36] To be sure, perceived threats to identity can outweigh real threats to either security or prosperity. In the next section, this hypothesis is applied to three of the modern world"s most enduring conflicts—Israel-Palestine, India-Pakistan, and China-Taiwan—to determine whether these seemingly irresolvable disputes are driven, today, predominantly by fear, by interest, or by honor.

Intractable Problems

Israel-Palestine: Under pressure from influential Zionists, Great Britain issued the Balfour Declaration of 1917, endorsing Palestine as "a national home for the Jewish people."[37] In 1923, the League of Nations established Palestine as a British mandate.

The preamble of the document that established the British Mandate of Palestine echoed the endorsement of the Balfour Declaration. Zionists began immigrating to Palestine in earnest. The significant expansion of Jews threatened the security and the prosperity of the Arab Palestinians.

Tensions between the Arabs, the Jews, and the British steadily increased until the Arab Revolt of 1936. According to Michael Gasper, this rebellion was "the midwife for the emergence of Palestinian nationalism… as large segments of the Palestinian public joined in the nationalist cause for the first time."[38] In 1947, Britain announced it would terminate the mandate, and the United Nations (UN) endorsed a plan to establish separate Jewish and Arab states with Jerusalem as an international enclave under UN control.[39] Israel would comprise approximately 55% of the land; Palestine would comprise 45%, and Jerusalem would comprise the other 5%.[40] The Zionists, with reservations, endorsed the plan. However, the Palestinians largely rejected it as inequitable, and violence between the two ensued. The UN plan was never implemented, as a wider war broke out between the Arabs and the Israelis.

On May 15, 1948, the British Mandatory Government left Jerusalem, the State of Israel declared independence, and the Arab armies of Egypt, Syria, and Jordan invaded. As Gasper notes, "Fortunately for the Israelis, these Arab armies not only lacked a unified command structure, but they also did not have unified war aims in mind."[41] They were each driven by their own national security, prosperity, and identity concerns.[42] During this opening round in the Arab-Israeli conflict, hundreds of thousands of Palestinians were displaced, and the participating Arab armies were disgraced. By the end, Israel controlled three-quarters of Palestine.[43] Despite, or perhaps because of this resounding victory, the security of Israel remained threatened, and Arab-Israeli tensions continued unabated. Dislocated and humiliated by a nascent Jewish state, the Palestinians and neighboring Arabs would struggle to reclaim lost land and lost pride. Israel, besieged by bitter Arab animosity, would endeavor to survive.

In 1956, Egypt closed the Straits of Tiran and the recently nationalized Suez Canal to Israeli shipping. The blockade posed a direct threat to Israeli prosperity. Israel, with British and French support, responded by invading and capturing Egypt"s Gaza Strip and Sinai Peninsula. Under U.S.-led UN pressure, Israel agreed to withdraw from Egyptian territory, and Egypt"s Arab-nationalist leader, Gamal Abdel Nasser, emerged as a hero. A decade later, Nasser"s identity as leader of the Arab world would force Egypt into a confrontation for which it and the rest of that world were ill prepared.

During the next decade, Palestinian nationalism was on the rise and armed squads of Palestinians attacked Israel from safe havens inside Syria.[44] Reciprocal attacks between Israel and Syria escalated, and in 1967, Israel threatened to strike Damascus. In response, Egypt, having recently signed a mutual defense agreement with Syria and Jordan, deployed forces into the Sinai and once again closed the Straits of Tiran to Israeli shipping. Israel responded to these threats with devastating air and ground offenses that, in just six days, wrested control of the Sinai Peninsula, the Gaza Strip, the West Bank, East Jerusalem, and the Golan Heights from the Arabs. According to Ann Lesh and Dan Tschirgi, the war would destroy Nasser"s credibility and cause "a seismic shock in the Middle East, equal to the impact of the fighting in 1948-1949."[45]

In 1973, Egypt and Syria, launching simultaneous attacks on the holiest day of the Jewish year, Yom Kippur, caught Israel off guard. With U.S. assistance, Israel was able to turn the tide and emerge victorious.[46] This war marked the last war between Israel and a combined Arab force.[47] Egypt and Israel signed a peace treaty in 1979. In reaction, nearly all of the other Arab states suspended diplomatic relations with Egypt.[48] Israel had disfigured the Arab self image and, for many, rapprochement was unthinkable. Nevertheless, the conflict largely shifted from the regional to the local level.

The Palestinians, completely disillusioned with the ability of the Arab states to succeed in the protracted struggle, turned to the Palestinian Liberation Organization (PLO) for leadership.[49] Throughout the next decade, Israel endeavored to defeat the PLO, which they blamed for the Palestinian unrest occurring in the Gaza Strip and the West Bank. In 1982, Israel invaded Lebanon multiple times in an effort to destroy the PLO"s political and military infrastructure. Impairing the PLO"s ability to lead resulted in the growth of autonomous resistance movements in the Palestinian territories.[50] The first major Palestinian uprising, or *Intifada*, in the territories began in 1987 and lasted for several years. It was a popular revolt that brought international attention and aid to the Palestinian plight. The Second Intifada began in 2000 with a series of Palestinian suicide bombings. Israel suppressed this more violent and extremist-led uprising with massive force.[51] Israel"s Gaza Strip and West Bank barriers, as well as its numerous West Bank checkpoints, limit Palestinian extremists" ability to inflict significant damage on Israel today. The conflict, however, remains unresolved. It is one that is shaped by and, at the same time, shapes and the identities of the actors involved.

According to Simona Sharoni and Mohammed Abu-Nimer, "The Palestinian-Israeli conflict has played a central role in shaping the collective identities of Palestinians and Jews."[52] These two authors and residents of the disputed region

13

contend that the conflict has "served as both the catalyst and the touchstone for the consolidation of particular notions of national „imagined community" for Palestinians and for Israeli Jews."[53] By examining this conflict, one may conclude that the Israeli identity arose from a sense of vulnerability and that the Palestinian identity arose from a sense of ignominy. As Sharoni and Abu-Nimer observe, the collective identity of the former emphasizes national security, and that of the latter emphasizes national liberation.[54]

Israel"s quest for national security is the impetus of Palestine"s quest for national liberation. In essence, Israeli repression engenders Palestinian rebellion and vice versa. The two are caught in an identity dilemma. Furthermore, Israel"s national security successes represent Arab nationalist failures. Arab honor has been impinged. Although the proximate cause of several rounds of armed conflict can be traced to security and prosperity, it is this identity dilemma that prolongs the conflict and complicates peace efforts. The collective identities, conceivably present early in the contest, were reinforced over time. Hardened identity has led to obdurate inflexibility on several sides of the interminable dispute. While the most protracted, this is not the only existing case of identity prolonging enmity.

India-Pakistan: Deep-seated differences over the status of Kashmir have led to an unresolved confrontation between India and Pakistan.[55] Located in the northwesternmost region of South Asia, where the borders of India, Pakistan, and China meet, Kashmir is a mountainous region of seven million people that is claimed by both India and Pakistan. The status of Kashmir has been in dispute since India and Pakistan were partitioned by the Indian Independence Act of 1947 because, as a Carter Center report on the conflict notes, "a plebiscite called for by the United Nations to discern

Kashmiri wishes about their political status was never held."[56] The 1947 partition immediately created conflict between the two nations.

Pakistan"s prosperity was threatened by the prospect of India controlling the main source of water for Pakistan"s cultivatable land: the Indus basin located in Kashmir. Seeking to avoid hostilities, the two signed a water-sharing agreement—the Indus Waters Treaty—in 1960. While the treaty has been upheld by both sides, it has not lead to an overall easing of tensions between the two countries. Kashmir is currently divided along the Line of Control (LOC), an undemarcated but de facto border established between India and Pakistan along the ceasefire line of 1971.[57] India maintains Kashmir is part of India and has built a complex barrier along the LOC. Pakistan believes its final status should be determined by the people of Kashmir and objects to the LOC barrier. According to the Central Intelligence Agency"s World Factbook, Kashmir, "remains the site of the world's largest and most militarized territorial dispute."[58] India and Pakistan have waged three wars—1947, 1965, and 1971 Indo-Pakistani Wars—and are purportedly engaged in an ongoing proxy war over the contested territory.

Lashkar-e-Taiba (LeT) is a banned radical Islamic group based near Lahore, Pakistan focused on establishing an Islamic state in Kashmir. According to the Council on Foreign Relations (CFR), "LeT is among several banned Pakistani militant groups that experts say received backing from Pakistan's intelligence agency, the Inter-Services Intelligence, to fight in Indian-administered Kashmir."[59] The CFR backgrounder goes on to note that "analysts say the group continues to operate freely inside Pakistan under a different name."[60] The Indian government blamed the group for the November 2008 assault in Mumbai that killed nearly two hundred people. The group poses a threat to the security of India and, given that an LeT assault on parliament in Delhi precipitated the 2001-2002 India-Pakistan standoff, it poses threat to the stability of South Asia. However, LeT, like other extremist organizations, is a product (or a proxy) but not a producer of conflict.

This incessant dispute is not about prosperity, nor is it about security. The conflict between India and Pakistan over the territory of Kashmir is now and has always been about identity. Like Israel and Palestine, these two adversaries are caught in an identity dilemma. At the root of the conflict, according to Chenoy, are the "contending nationalisms" of Pakistan and India.[61] Pakistan was founded upon the belief that a separate country was necessary because Muslims would be oppressed under a Hindu-majority rule. Ceding the Muslim-majority Kashmir to India poses a threat to Pakistan"s foundational identity.[62] Conversely, ceding the Muslim-majority territory to Muslim-majority Pakistan "represents a defeat of India"s secularism."[63] A Georgetown University Berkley Center for Religion, Peace, & World Affairs case study on Kashmir echoes this assessment: "At the root of the conflict are the nationalist movements of each country and the evolution of these movements since independence."[64] According to Stephen Cohen, there are two Kashmirs.[65] His assessment is enlightening and, thus, merits reiterating:

> Besides the physical territory, another Kashmir is found in the minds of politicians, strategists, soldiers and ideologues. This is a place where national and sub-national identities are ranged against each other. The conflict in this Kashmir is as much a clash between identities, imagination, and history, as it is a conflict over territory, resources and peoples.[66]

Shankar Bajpai, too, is convinced the conflict is one of identity.[67] Because identity is at stake, solving the conflict will be difficult, if not impossible, unless perceptions regarding identity change. According to Cohen, "There can be no real peace process between

16

India and Pakistan as long as either retains its identity."[68] These opposing and evolving identities reinforce one another and prolong the dispute. Identity is also a significant factor in the last conflict examined in this essay.

China-Taiwan: Taiwan, incorporated into the Chinese Qing dynasty in the 17th century, was annexed and ruled by Japan from 1895 to 1945. At the end of World War II, China, under the Kuomintang (KMT) or Republic of China (ROC) government, reacquired control of Taiwan from Japan. Four years later, at the end of the Chinese Civil War, the ROC government lost control of mainland China to the Communist Party of China and moved to the island of Taiwan. The People's Republic of China (PRC) was born and the nation was divided in two: the PRC (China) and the ROC (Taiwan).

Today, China is Taiwan's largest trading partner and, while the economic and social interaction across the strait is, as Richard Bush notes, "broad and deep," China and Taiwan have never formally recognized each other"s sovereignty.[69] Chinese reunification is the official policy of China. According to B.J. Jordan, "The concept of „One-China" has been part of Chinese political orthodoxy since ancient times. Often, if one claimed to be emperor of China with the mandate of heaven, all the other regimes within the country were either rebel or tributary."[70] One China reunification requires that the mainland territories controlled by China and the island territories controlled by Taiwan be brought under a single political entity. While unification is China"s goal, Taiwan"s goal increasingly appears to be independence.

As Sheila Jager notes, "Taiwan is already a de facto independent state, albeit one without international recognition."[71] Formal recognition of Taiwan"s independence, as she observes, threatens China"s territorial integrity:

A declaration of de jure independence by Taiwan would... constitute a real threat to the territorial integrity of China, since it could invite a dynamic of national disintegration... After all, provinces like Tibet and Xinjiang, with their own distinct ethnicity, language, and culture, have much stronger claims to separate national identity than Taiwan with its majority Han population.[72]

Yet, in Taiwan, there is a growing sense of a separate Taiwanese identity driving the country"s quest for recognition.[73]

This emerging Taiwanese identity has been propelling the island towards a clash with mainland China. From 2000 to 2008, Taiwan"s Democratic Progressive Party (DPP) sought formal recognition of Taiwan's sovereignty from the international community. In response to such efforts, as a CFR backgrounder on the conflict notes, "China has deployed ballistic missiles along the Taiwan Strait and continues to modernize both its missile forces and its amphibious assault capabilities."[74] In 2008, Taiwan"s KMT, led by President Ma, assumed power from the DPP and took a more conciliatory approach toward China.[75] Nevertheless, identity can and does strain the bilateral relationship.

Melissa Brown concludes that "Ultimately the problem is one of identity—Han ethnic Chinese, Chinese national identity, and the relationship of both of these identities to the new Taiwanese identity forged in the 1990s."[76] The budding Taiwanese identity has strengthened, as China has acted to suppress it.[77] Indeed, as Brown notes, China"s threats serve to consolidate Taiwan"s independent identity.[78] What Brown does not offer though is that the reverse is also occurring; Taiwan"s displays of independence serve to strengthen China"s nationalistic goal of reunifying the state. Collective identity is a powerful force. As Bush observes, "the [Taiwanese] leadership sometimes feels constrained by nationalistic pressures from the public."[79] The CFR backgrounder observes that "Since the KMT was elected to power in 2008, President Ma's rapprochement with Beijing has incited pro-independence protests."[80] Today, cross-strait relations between China and Taiwan appear calm on the surface, but because of emerging identity, may one day become violent.

The Consequence of Identity

The three cases examined in the previous section indicate that, over time, identity becomes the most significant of the three motives for continuing a confrontation. In addition to security and prosperity, the reputation of the state—its people and leaders—is wagered during conflict. The distinct image of self held and projected by the society is at stake. As a result, the conflict becomes firmly associated with self-esteem. Rhetoric reinforces this association, and as the passions of the populace are enflamed, the flexibility of the leadership becomes constrained.[81]

Simply stated, the analysis suggests that honor is stronger than fear or interest as a motive for prolonging conflict. Identities in conflict are modified over time in reaction to one another. Each identity threatens the other, and an identity dilemma, similar to a security dilemma, unfolds. The analysis suggests, then, that societies in conflict will eventually endeavor to maintain identity at the expense of security (blood) and prosperity (treasure). The relationship between the three may be depicted as an equilateral triangle with security (S), prosperity (P), and identity (I) residing at the vertices. At the outset of conflict, any of the three motives may be the more significant (or proximate) and, thus, reside at the top. Over time, however, the significance of identity increases and, ultimately, it rises to the apex of the triangle (see Figure below).

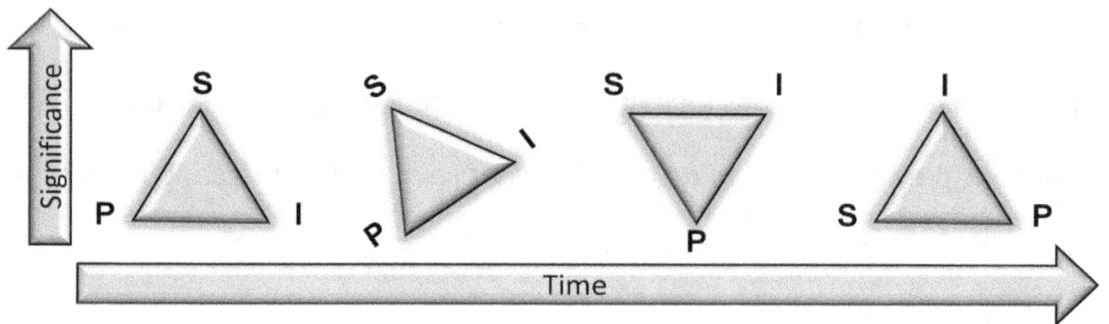

At the outset of conflict, depicted by the first triangle, security may be more significant than prosperity and identity [S>(P=I)]. As time progresses, identity, while not as significant as security, becomes more significant than prosperity (S>I>P). Soon, identity becomes as significant as security and both are more important than prosperity [(I=S)>P]. Finally, identity becomes more significant than security and prosperity [I>(S=P)].

Identities in conflict solidify over time in relation and reaction to one another. Each one of the identity dilemmas examined here possesses the potential for full-scale war. Such wars, in which the total resources of the belligerents may be employed, can prove devastating for all parties involved. If identity resides at the core of all three of the world"s most potentially catastrophic conflicts, it must be an integral part of the contemplated solutions. The next section examines a recently developed governmental approach to analyzing conflict that regards threats to identity as core grievances meriting careful consideration.

<u>Honorable Solutions</u>

The Interagency Conflict Assessment Framework (ICAF) was created by a United States government interagency working group co-chaired by the U.S. Department of State"s Office of the Coordinator for Stabilization and Reconstruction and United States Aid and International Development"s Office of Conflict Management and Mitigation.[82] The ICAF draws on existing social science methodologies for analyzing and resolving conflict. The first major task in the ICAF process is to diagnose the conflict. Step one of the diagnosis is evaluating the context of the conflict. Step two is understanding the core grievances. Step three is identifying the drivers of conflict, and step four is describing the prospects for alleviating as well as aggravating the conflict. The second major task in the analysis is preparing for conflict intervention.[83]

Step two of diagnosing the conflict—understanding core grievances—calls for describing the threatened identity groups. According to the ICAF, "Identity groups are inclined to conflict when they perceive that other groups" interests, needs and aspirations compete with and jeopardize their identity, security or other fundamental interests."[84] These threats clearly correspond to the triad of motives for conflict described here. What the ICAF does not do, but this examination advocates, is elevate threats to identity above threats to security or prosperity. The ICAF is a sound process for analyzing conflict. The analysis above suggests, however, that ontological security is more important than physical and fiscal security. Jennifer Mitzen, too, contends that "ontological security-seeking sheds new light on seemingly irrational conflict."[85] Emphasizing identity may enhance the accuracy and efficacy of the ICAF.

The present examination is not alone in advocating the elevation of identity as a catalyst for and cornerstone of conflict. The U.S. Army War College recently developed an "Analytical Cultural Framework for Strategy and Policy" (ACFSP) to illuminate the cultural dimensions that drive strategic behavior.[86] According to a Strategic Studies Institute (SSI) paper on the ACFSP, these dimensions are identity, political culture, defined as "the structure of power and decision-making,"[87] and resilience or "the capacity or ability to resist, adapt, or succumb to external forces."[88] Of the three, the SSI paper contends that identity may, in fact, be the most important driver.[89] Identity, although perhaps unexamined by the contending parties, is often central to the conflict and, thus, integral to a negotiated solution.

In their national bestseller *Getting to Yes*, Roger Fisher and William Ury encourage negotiators to focus on "interests, not positions" to resolve disputes.[90] These interests are the basic, often unstated concerns behind a given position.[91] James Sebenius describes these interests as "the underlying concerns of deeper dimensions of value that would be affected by different resolution of the issues under negotiation."[92] However, as George Woods notes in "The Strategic Leader as Negotiator," these concerns are often not consciously examined.[93] Finding a mutually agreeable alternative position becomes possible only when the underlying concerns of the opposing parties become clear.[94] Those seeking negotiated solutions should regard identity, although often unstated, as one of the most important factors in any conflict.

At the root of the world"s most stubborn conflicts, identity dilemmas are found. Solutions that consider identity (honor) above security (fear) and prosperity (interest) may hold promise for resolving seemingly intractable conflicts. Honorable solutions aim to redress legitimate grievances without diminishing the honor, threatening the identity, or damaging the esteem of the parties involved. Indeed, honorable solutions seek, first and foremost, to bolster honor while addressing fears and interests. Such solutions are not easily devised, but may be entirely necessary to defuse mankind"s most dangerous disputes.

Taking the Triad Further

A single line in a serendipitous speech delivered on the eve of the Peloponnesian War, over two thousand years ago, succinctly articulates the primary motives for human conflict. In the line, the three major forces—physical, material, and social—that

22

influence individual and collective behavior are articulated. In the line, the three major paradigms of international relations theory are represented: realism through fear, liberalism through interest, and constructivism through honor. In *Leviathan*, Hobbes labeled the three motives explored here as competition, diffidence, and glory. According to Hobbes, "The first, maketh men invade for gain; the second, for safety; and the third, for reputation."[95] These motives may be constants, but their relative weight is influenced by culture.

Cultural values shape how societies perceive themselves, others, and their environment. These values influence how members of a society think and act. Profound cultural awareness facilitates comprehending the relationship between security, prosperity, and identity within a society. These three motives compel states, as constructs of man, to compete and, thus, to conflict. Identity, as argued here, often outweighs both security and prosperity as a motive, and so should be given greater emphasis in analyzing and resolving conflict. Determining the relative importance of the latter two motives would add merit to this basic premise. Establishing the relationship between the motives offers a method for classifying the collective identity, and, perhaps, for accurately extrapolating the strategic behavior of the state. However, doing so requires a more extensive exploration of the cultures in conflict than undertaken in this initial endeavor. Such strategic identity typologies, while not exhaustive, impart broader explanatory power to the triad and, though beyond the scope of the present examination, warrant further consideration.

Endnotes

[1] Thucydides, *The Landmark Thucydides: A Comprehensive Guide to the Peloponnesian War*, trans. Robert Strassler (New York: Free Press, 1996), 43. According to Lebow, the "case"

23

in question consists of the Corcyraean alliance, the siege of Potidaea, and the Megarian Decree. Thucydides may not have been making a general statement regarding the significance of fear, interest, and honor. Yet, these three words arguably capture the primary motives for human conflict. See Richard Ned Lebow, *A Cultural Theory of International Relations* (Cambridge: Cambridge University Press, 2008), 160.

[2] Richard Ned Lebow, *A Cultural Theory of International Relations* (Cambridge: Cambridge University Press, 2008), 509.

[3] Thomas Hobbes, *Leviathan*, (Printed for Andrew Crooke, at the Green Dragon in St. Paul's Churchyard, 1651), Chapter VIII, http://oregonstate.edu/instruct/phl302/texts/hobbes/leviathan-contents.html (accessed December 10, 2010).

[4] Hobbes, *Leviathan*, Chapter VIII.

[5] For more on political realism, see Hans Morgenthau, *Politics Among Nations* (New York: Knopf, 1948).

[6] Kenneth N. Waltz, "The Origins of War in Neorealist Theory," *Journal of Interdisciplinary History* 18, no. 4 (Spring 1988), 616.

[7] Ibid., 620.

[8] Joseph S. Nye, Jr. and David A. Welch, *Understanding Global Conflict and Cooperation: An Introduction to Theory and History* (Boston: Longman, 2009), 17.

[9] Daniel Tompkins, "Fear, Honor and Profit?: Ambiguity and Ideation in Thucydides" Athenian Speech," Paper presented at the annual meeting of the American Political Science Association, Philadelphia, PA, August 31, 2006. May 24, 2009, http://www.allacademic.com/meta/p150688_index.html (accessed December 12, 2010).

[10] Waltz, "The Origins of War," 620.

[11] Thucydides, *The Landmark Thucydides*, 16.

[12] Nye and Welch, *Understanding Global Conflict and Cooperation*, 20.

[13] For more on the results of cooperation, see Robert Axelrod, *The Evolution of Cooperation* (New York: Basic Books, 2006).

[14] John Locke, *The Second Treatise of Government*, Chapter III, Section 21, 1690, http://www.gutenberg.org/files/7370/7370-h/7370-h.htm (accessed December 12, 2010).

[15] Immanuel Kant, "Perpetual Peace," in *Immanuel Kant: On History*, ed. and trans. Lewis White Beck (Upper Saddle River, NJ: Prentice Hall 1964) reprinted in *Conflict After the Cold War*, ed. Richard K. Betts (New York: Longman, 2002), 103.

[16] James Nathan, *Soldiers, Statecraft, and History: Coercive Diplomacy and International Order* (Westport: Praeger, 2002). Nathan examines the historical use of force within the

international arena to draw lessons and to derive present-day national security policy prescriptions. The thrust of his argument is that the use of force, while an effective tool of the state, should be limited in purpose and scope. Used otherwise, force may prove self-defeating.

[17] Jeffrey S. Lantis, "Strategic Culture and National Security Policy," *International Studies Review* 4, no. 3 (Autumn, 2002), 91.

[18] Alexander Wendt, "Constructing International Politics," *International Security* 20, no. 1 (Summer, 1995), 81.

[19] Lebow, *A Cultural Theory*, 505.

[20] Ibid., 505.

[21] Lebow acknowledges that this an ideal-type and not a real-type where all three motives are likely to be at work.

[22] Lebow, *A Cultural Theory*, 167.

[23] Ibid.,168.

[24] Ibid., 516.

[25] Thucydides, *The Landmark Thucydides*, 39.

[26] Ibid., 38.

[27] Lebow, *A Cultural Theory*, 180.

[28] Ibid., 180. For an exceptional examination of ontological security-seeking behavior and how rational security-seekers could become attached to conflict, see Jennifer Mitzen, "Ontological Security in World Politics: State Identity and the Security Dilemma," *European Journal of International Relations* 12, no. 3 (September, 2006), 341-370.

[29] James Bowman, *Honor: A History* (New York: Encounter Books, 2006), 6.

[30] Richard Ned Lebow, "Fear, Interest and Honour: Outlines of a Theory of International Relations," *International Affairs* 82, no. 3 (May, 2006), 431.

[31] Ronald L. Jepperson, Alexander Wendt, and Peter J. Katzenstein, "Norms, Identity, and Culture in National Security," in *The Culture of National Security: Norms and Identity in World Politics* (New York: Columbia University Press, 1996), 59.

[32] Ibid.

[33] All one need do to confirm the validity of these statements is note the 2010 United States National Security Strategy"s "enduring national interests" headings entitled "Security," "Prosperity," and "Values." Barak Obama, *National Security Strategy 2010* (Washington, DC: The White House, May 2010), 18.

[34] "The growth of Athens, and the alarm which this inspired in Sparta, made war inevitable." Thucydides, *The Landmark Thucydides*, 16.

[35] Lebow, *A Cultural Theory*, 180.

[36] Athens" arguably imprudent actions over the course of the conflict appear to have been motivated by identity as well.

[37] The full text of the statement reads "His Majesty's Government view with favor the establishment in Palestine of a national home for the Jewish people, and will use their best endeavors to facilitate the achievement of this object, it being clearly understood that nothing shall be done which may prejudice the civil and religious rights of existing non-Jewish communities in Palestine, or the rights and political status enjoyed by Jews in any other country." Modern History Sourcebook, "The Balfour Declaration," http://www.fordham.edu/halsall/mod/balfour.html (accessed March 18, 2011).

[38] Michael Gasper, "The Making of the Modern Middle East," in *The Middle East*, ed. Ellen Lust (Washington: CQ Press, 2011), 36.

[39] United Nations General Assembly Resolution 181.

[40] Ann M. Lesh and Dan Tschirgi, *Origins and Development of the Arab Israeli Conflict*, (Westport: Greenwood Press, 1998),10.

[41] Gasper, "Making the Middle East," 37.

[42] For a brief examination of the various motives, see Gasper, 37.

[43] Lesh and Tschirgi, *Origins and Development*, 11-12.

[44] Ibid., 20.

[45] Ibid., 21.

[46] Ibid., 25.

[47] Simona Sharoni and Mohammed Abu-Nimer, "The Israeli Palestinian Conflict" in *Understanding the Contemporary Middle East*, ed. Jillian Schwedler and Deborah J. Gerner (Boulder: Lynne Rienner, 2008), 191.

[48] Lesh and Tschirgi, *Origins and Development*, 30.

[49] Sharoni and Abu-Nimer, "The Israeli Palestinian Conflict," 191.

[50] Ibid., 194.

[51] Ibid., 200.

[52] Ibid., 179.

[53] Ibid., 202.

[54] Ibid., 203.

[55] K. Shankar Bajpai, "Untangling India and Pakistan," *Foreign Affairs* 82, No. 3. May/June 2003, http://www.foreignaffairs.com/articles/58979/k-shankar-bajpai/untangling-india-and-pakistan (accessed February 28, 2011).

[56] The Carter Center, "The Kashmiri Conflict: Historical and Prospective Intervention Analyses," July 2003, www.cartercenter.org/documents/1439.pdf (accessed March, 6 2011), 4.

[57] Another ceasefire line, known as the Line of Actual Control, separates the Indian-controlled area from the Chinese-controlled area.

[58] Central Intelligence Agency, World Factbook, https://www.cia.gov/library/publications/the-world-factbook/geos/pk.html (accessed February 28, 2011).

[59] Council on Foreign Relations, "Backgrounder: Lashkar-e-Taiba," http://www.cfr.org/pakistan/lashkar-e-taiba-army-pure-aka-lashkar-e-tayyiba-lashkar-e-toiba-lashkar--taiba/p17882 (accessed March 6, 2011).

[60] Ibid.

[61] Kamal Chenoy, "Contending Nationalisms," *Harvard International Review* 28, no. 3, (Fall, 2006), 24.

[62] Ibid., 24.

[63] Ibid., 24.

[64] Georgetown University, "Kashmir: Religious Diversity becomes Religious Militancy," *Berkley Center for Religion, Peace, & World Affairs Case Study Series*, July 2009, http://repository.berkleycenter.georgetown.edu/KashmirConflictCaseStudy.pdf (accessed March 6, 2011).

[65] Stephen Philip Cohen, "India, Pakistan and Kashmir," *Journal of Strategic Studies* 25, no. 4 (June, 2010), 45.

[66] Ibid., 45-46.

[67] Bajpai, "Untangling India and Pakistan."

[68] Cohen, "India, Pakistan and Kashmir," 53.

[69] Richard C. Bush, *Untying the Knot: Making Peace in the Taiwan Strait* (Washington, DC: Brookings Institute Press, 2005), 4.

[70] B.J. Jordan, "China and the Far East," in *The Ashgate Research Companion to U.S. Foreign Policy*, ed. Robert J Pauly, Jr., (Burlington, VT: Ashgate Publishing, 2010), 181.

[71] Sheila Miyoshi Jager, "The Politics of Identity: History, Nationalism, and the Prospects for Peace in Post-Cold War East Asia," Strategic Studies Institute, April 2007,

http://www.strategicstudiesinstitute.army.mil/pubs/display.cfm?pubID=770 (accessed December 15, 2010), 24.

[72] Ibid., 25.

[73] Bush, *Untying the Knot*, 341.

[74] Council on Foreign Relations, "Backgrounder: China-Taiwan Relations," http://www.cfr.org/china/china-taiwan-relations/p9223 (accessed March 6, 2011).

[75] Ibid.

[76] Melissa J. Brown, *Is Taiwan Chinese?* (Berkley: University of California Press, 2004), 1.

[77] Ibid., 241.

[78] Ibid., 240.

[79] Bush, *Untying the Knot*, 342.

[80] Council of Foreign Relations, "China Taiwan Relations."

[81] Lesh and Tschirgi, *Origins and Development*, 11.

[82] The working group included representatives from the Office of the Secretary of Defense, U.S. Joint Forces Command and the U.S. Army"s Peacekeeping and Stability Operations Institute. United States Department of State, "Interagency Conflict Assessment Framework" (Washington, DC: Office of the Coordinator for Reconstruction and Stabilization).

[83] Ibid.

[84] According to the ICAF, identity groups are "people that identify with each other, often on the basis of characteristics used by outsiders to describe them (e.g., ethnicity, race, nationality, religion, political affiliation, age, gender, economic activity or socio-economic status)." Ibid.

[85] Mitzen, "Ontological Security," 341.

[86] Jiyul Kim, "Cultural Dimensions of Strategy and Policy," Strategic Studies Institute, May 2009, www.strategicstudiesinstitute.army.mil/pdffiles/PUB919.pdf mil/ (accessed December 15, 2010), 9.

[87] Ibid., 10.

[88] Ibid.

[89] Ibid., 15.

[90] Roger Fisher and William Ury, *Getting to Yes: Negotiating Agreement without Giving In* (New York: Penguin, 1991), 40.

[91] Ibid., 40.

[92] James Sebenius, *Introduction to Negotiation Analysis: Creating and Claiming Value* (Boston: Harvard Business School Press, 1997), 3.

[93] George Woods, "The Strategic Leader as Negotiator" in *Strategic Leadership: The General's Art* (Vienna, Virginia: Management Concepts, 2009), 233.

[94] Fisher and Ury, *Getting to Yes*, 42.

[95] Hobbes, *Leviathan*, Chapter VIII.

www.ingramcontent.com/pod-product-compliance
Lightning Source LLC
Chambersburg PA
CBHW081810280526
45789CB00008B/3079